Amazing Americans: Abraham Lincoln

Stephanie Kuligowski, M.A.T.

Consultants

Shelley Scudder
Gifted Education Teacher
Broward County Schools

Caryn Williams, M.S.Ed.
Madison County Schools
Huntsville, AL

Publishing Credits

Dona Herweck Rice, *Editor-in-Chief*
Lee Aucoin, *Creative Director*
Torrey Maloof, *Editor*
Diana Kenney, M.A.Ed., NBCT, *Associate Education Editor*
Marissa Rodriguez, *Designer*
Stephanie Reid, *Photo Editor*
Rachelle Cracchiolo, M.S.Ed., Publisher

Image Credits: Cover & p. 1 Alamy; pp. 4, 6, 12, 13 North Wind Picture Archives; pp. 8, 9, 10, 15, 16, 24 The Granger Collection; p. 3 The Library of Congress [LC-USZC2-2917]; p. 5 The Library of Congress [LC-DIG-ppmsca-19305]; p. 7 The Library of Congress [LC-DIG-ggbain-21723]; p. 11 The Library of Congress [LC-DIG-ppmsca-19241]; p. 14 The Library of Congress [LC-B8171-7929; p. 20 The Library of Congress [LC-DIG-pga-00380]; All other images from Shutterstock.

Teacher Created Materials
5301 Oceanus Drive
Huntington Beach, CA 92649-1030
http://www.tcmpub.com

ISBN 978-1-4333-6981-0

Table of Contents

President Lincoln 4

Country Boy 6

On His Own 10

Saving America 12

He Did It! 18

Amazing Americans Today 20

Glossary 22

Index 23

Your Turn! 24

President Lincoln

Abraham Lincoln (LING-kuhn) was America's 16th **president**. He was born in 1809. His parents called him Abe.

This is Abe and his family when he was president.

Honest Abe

Lincoln was called *Honest Abe*. People say he always told the truth.

Country Boy

Abe's parents were **pioneers** in Kentucky. They were farmers.

Abe's family lived in a log cabin. They were poor.

A young Abe cuts wood for his mother.

The Lincoln family lived in this log cabin.

Abe helped his family on the farm most of the day. Abe also spent hours reading. He loved books.

Abe reads as a child at home.

Abe reads as a grown-up while he works.

On His Own

Abe did not want to be a farmer. He became a **lawyer**. He loved to help people.

Abe works as a lawyer.

Funny Man

Abe told lots of funny stories.
People liked him.

Abe Lincoln

Saving America

Abe thought **slavery** was wrong. Many people agreed. They **elected** him president in 1860.

President Abraham Lincoln

Unfair!

Slaves are people who are forced to work without pay. They have no **freedom**.

These slaves are working in a field.

Abe was president during the Civil War. It started in 1861. Abe worked hard to free America from slavery.

Abe meets with army leaders.

The Civil War

In the Civil War, America split into two parts. The North and South fought against each other.

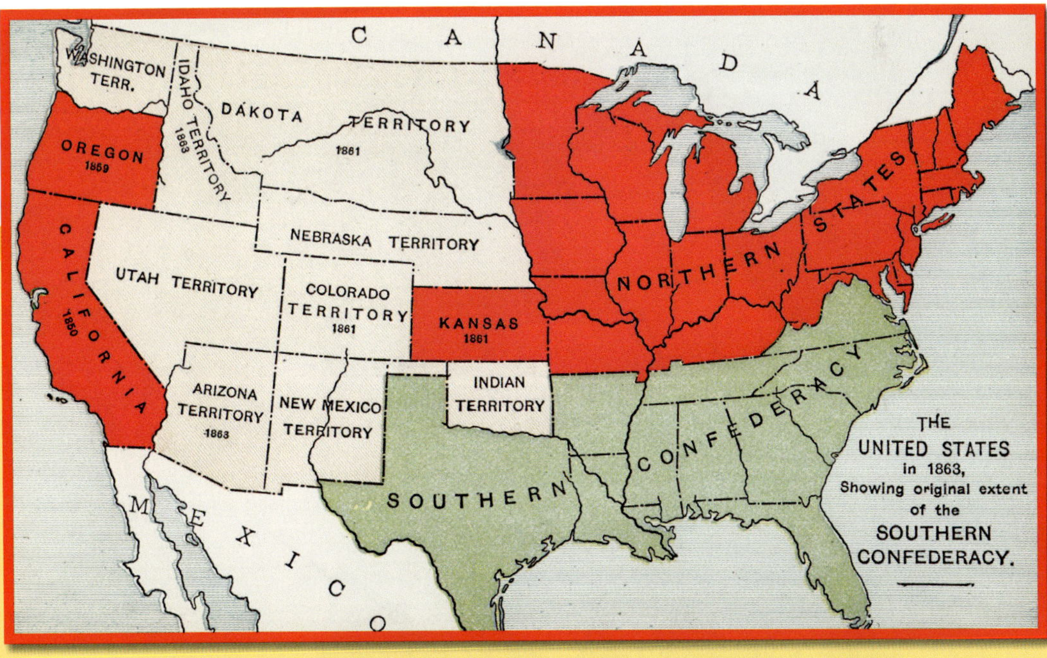

The Northern states are red.
The Southern states are green.

The North did not think slavery was right. The South wanted to keep slaves. The two sides fought for four years!

The South fights the North in the Civil War.

Famous Speech

Abe gave a **speech** in 1863. It was called the Gettysburg (GET-iz-burg) Address. Today, it is one of the most famous speeches in the world.

He Did It!

Lincoln did it! He kept America together. He freed the slaves. Many people call him the greatest American president.

This is a statue of Abe Lincoln.

An Honor

Abe has been **honored** with many statues. His face is also on the five dollar bill and the penny!

Amazing Americans Today

Abraham Lincoln was an amazing American. He worked hard to help people.

Today, there are many amazing Americans. They work hard to help people, too.

This is Joey and his cousin Zac.

Draw It!

Draw a picture of an amazing American you know. Tell why this person is amazing.

Joey drew this picture of Zac. Zac works hard to help people and the land. He grew and took care of plants in a place that needed it.

Glossary

elected—chosen for a job by votes

freedom—the power to do what you want to do

honored—shown respect

lawyer—a person who helps people with the law

pioneers—the first people to move to a new area

president—leader of a country

slavery—being owned by another person and forced to work without pay

slaves—people who are forced to work without pay and have no freedom

speech—a public talk

Index

Civil War, 14–16

Gettysburg Address, 17

Kentucky, 6

lawyer, 10

pioneers, 6

president, 4, 12, 14, 18

slavery, 12–14, 16, 18

Your Turn!

He Loved to Read

Abraham Lincoln loved to read. Look at the picture above. Why do you think Abe read so much? How do you think it helped him?